GENTLEPRENEUR

SERENITY & SUCCESS

HARSH BHARTI

Contents

PREFACE

ॐ

I'm **19 years old**, still figuring things out, and not yet where I want to be in life. But one thing I have realized is that success isn't about hard work or big goals—it's a blend of **mindset, discipline, and belief** in something bigger than yourself.

I started this journey like many others, full of ambition but unsure, hustling endlessly, yet feeling lost. That's when I realized the real game-changer wasn't just working harder—it was a combination of **clarity, discipline, resilience, and inner peace**. Without these, even the biggest achievement can feel empty.

This book **isn't a lecture**—I'm not writing it as someone who has already "made it" in life. It's a guide from someone who is **still on the journey**, learning and growing every day. This book is a reflection of what I've learned—practical business strategies mixed with **spiritual wisdom**—because I believe success isn't just about building a strong foundation externally but also within yourself.

Most people separate business and personal growth. We think success is only about external achievements—building wealth, getting promotions, starting a business.

But what I've learned is that **inner success is just as important**—your **mindset, habits, relationships, and even spiritual connection** all play a role in whether you truly succeed or not.

This book is for those who know they are meant for more but feel lost on how to get there. It's for those who want to build something meaningful—whether it's a **career or a better version of themselves**. My goal isn't to give you **unrealistic motivation** or overnight success formulas. My goal is to give you **practical strategies** that actually work—things you can apply in your daily life, whether you're a **student, an entrepreneur, or just someone trying to figure out their path**.

Success isn't just about reaching a **destination**—it's about **becoming the kind of person who can handle success when it comes.** If you're willing to grow, adapt, and stay consistent, success will follow.

17 March 2025

Acknowledgements

Every journey is shaped by the people who walk beside us, and this book is no exception. I owe my deepest gratitude to my parents, whose constant support, encouragement, endless sacrifices, and silent strength have been the foundation of my growth.

Second, I am grateful—thanks to my friends and colleagues. who have encouraged me along the way. Their motivation and constant support have played a vital role in shaping this book.

Lastly, to every reader—thank you for investing your time in these pages. May this book inspire you to push beyond limits and stay committed to your journey.

Prologue

Success is something we all dream about, but most of us struggle to figure out how to actually achieve it. Some think it's all about working non-stop, while others believe luck plays the biggest role. But if we look closely, success isn't just about making money, getting famous, or reaching a certain position. It's about growing as a person, building strong habits, and staying true to a purpose that goes beyond just personal gain.

This book is divided into different sections, each focusing on a key part of the journey. The first section talks about developing the right mindset for entrepreneurship—how to set clear goals, manage time effectively, and build strong relationships. The second section dives into the spiritual side of success—finding inner peace, overcoming struggles, and understanding the role of faith in staying strong. The third section is all about habits—how daily routines and small actions can shape your long-term success. Finally, the last section ties everything together, helping you stay focused on your journey without losing sight of what truly matters.

If you're someone who wants to do something big in life but sometimes feels lost or stuck, this book is for you. I hope these words help you find clarity, stay motivated, and, most importantly, believe in your own journey. Because at the end of the day, success isn't about reaching one final destination—it's about becoming a better version of yourself every single day.

"Don't be afrid to give up the good to go for the great"
~ Jhon.D.Rockefeller

● xi ●

I
Goal Setting

"Success begins with clarity. Every great achievement starts with well define goal" Without clear destination, even the most powerful ship will drip aimlessly at sea. In this chapter, we will explore why setting goal essential, how create meaningful objectives and strategies to turn your aspiration into reality.

First you have to set your goals. what you want from life and what are the things you want to achieve. Without any purpose or aim in life, life is nothing. Human are born to be success and achieve everything they want. Goal setting is your first motive and, also set a purpose for achieving your goal why you want to achieving your goal if you "why" are clear then nothing will stop you, if your purpose isn't clear then sometimes you feel aimlessly.

But simply setting your goal is not enough. Achieving success requires more than just knowing what you want to do. You need to build a strong foundation based on clarity commitment and action. Setting a goal with purpose is likely having map for your journey – without it, you might end up lost even if you are working hard.

Importance of goal setting

If you are trying to hit target and you can't see it would be nearly impossible. Goals provide direction purpose and motivation. They act as a road map, guiding you through challenges and obstacles. In business, having clear goals ensure you are not just working hard but working smart.

However, setting goals is not just about ambition. Its about aligning your actions with greater purpose. when your goal connects with your inner values, they ignite you passion making the journey more valuable and fulfilling.

The journey of book writing is an ambitious and transformative endeavor. Whether you are setting out to write first novel, an autobiography or self-help book. The process of writing book is overwhelming. But what if you could approach this momentum fascinating task with a clear plan, a serious of smaller manageable step and a road map that keeps you focused and motivated.

This is where the power of goal setting comes in. it is the tool that helps you to break down the idea of writing book into achievable measurable actions that can helps you on track.

~ *Set effective writing goals.*

Effective goal setting involves more than just thinking "I want to write a book" to ensure your goals are motivating, sustainable and lead to successful competition of your manuscript. They must be specific, measurable, achievable relevant and time bound. This is where the smart goal framework comes.

The power of clarity

Many people struggle to achieve success because their goals are vague saying. "I want to be rich" or "I want to be succeeded" lack of specificity. Instead of this ask yourself.

~ what does success mean to me?

~ How will I measure progress?

~ Why this goal is important for me?

Clarity transforms goal into actionable plans.

<u>For example,</u> instead of "I want to start a business" you might say "I want to launch a fintech or edtech startup that generates $10000 revenue within a year. this type of statement clears a goal. And create a Clarity in your vision.

The set of effective goals consider the **SMART** framework.

Specific ~ What exactly you want to achieve?

Measurable ~ How will you treat progress?

Achievable Ĩs the goal realistic?

Relevant ~Does it align with your values and long-term vision?

Time relevant ~ what your deadline?

Visualization.

Big goals can feel overwhelming. The keythings in that's break them into smaller and achievable goals. This type of approach can't build success in one day, but it makes progress and builds momentum.

For example, if your goal is to write a book starts with these steps:

- Outline the start.
- Write 500 words daily.
- Edit one chapter daily.

Small wins fuel motivation. Celebrate each milestone to keep yourself inspired.

Visualization is a powerful tool in a goal setting picture yourself achieving your goal. How does it feel? What does it look like? Visualization creates a mental image that enforce your believe system. Pair this, with affirmation. Visualization is a tool that can shape your reality. It is the act of mentally picturing your goals as already achieved. When you consistently visualize success, your mind starts to believe it is possible, aligning your thoughts and actions toward making it real.

The brain does not distinguish between real and vividly imagined experiences. Athletes, entrepreneurs, and high achievers use this technique to prepare themselves for success. When you see yourself succeeding in your mind, you develop the confidence and motivation to take the necessary steps in real life.

To make visualization effective, be specific. Picture the details—where you are, what you see, how you feel. Engage all your senses. If your goal is to start a business, imagine the office space, the clients, and the sound of success. Feel the excitement of achievement. Most importantly, combine visualization with action. Dreaming alone won't get you there; use it to fuel your determination.

Take a few minutes daily to close your eyes and see your success. The more vividly you visualize, the more your subconscious mind works to turn it into reality. Visualization is not magic—it is a tool to program your mind for success. Use it wisely.

Align your goals with inner self.

When you align your goal with your inner values. it ensures that your goal is not only materialistic things but also inner fulfillment and that resonate deeply your purpose of your character.

When your goal reflects your inner value, they become purposeful work that shape your character. In this journey you revel your deeper values, honesty, service, gratitude, compassion, or person growth. Aligning goals with these value that ensure your efforts contribute both external success and inner success.

When your goal aligning with your purpose. Then they prioritize your ambitions.

setting goal is the first step toward success, but achieving them requires dedication and perseverance. Remove all the obstacles which comes between you and your goal, whether they are emotional, mental and keep moving forward.

The main goal or purpose of your life should go beyond personal gain. It should be involving the helping the other people, contributing to society and making a positive impact on the world. This is not just way to succeed it is the way to live. You create a life where success is not measured by what you achieve but by the difference you make in the life of others.

--------- *Chapter summary* ----------

- Goal setting is the foundation of success it provides clarity, direction and purpose.
- Align your goals with your values or purpose that reflect your inner self.
- Know your "why" to stay motivated. A clear purpose makes you ahead even during challenges
- Set realistic goals, actionable goal and break big goals in smaller one.
- Remove all the obstacles that block your progress either its emotional or physical.
- Focus on helping others and contributing society and making the impact on the world.
- Find joy in the journey not just the destination.

II

The Time Edge

Time is the most valuable asset we have, yet it is often the most wasted. Unlike money or other resources, time can't be earned back. Every individual has the same 24 hours in a day, but it truly depends on how we use those hours that define our level of success. Time management is not about being busy, but it's all about using your time in an effective manner and focusing on what truly matters.

Effective time management leads to productivity, reduced stress, and discipline, which helps in a clear vision & purpose. By organizing time wisely, you can dedicate energy to your most important priorities, whether it's growing business, nurturing relationships, or focusing on personal growth. This skill is vital for entrepreneurs who often juggle multiple responsibilities and challenges.

In today's world, distractions are everywhere. Social media, constant notifications make it difficult to stay focused on what truly matters. Studies reveal that the average person spends 2-3 hours per day or more in scrolling through social media or engaging in unproductive tasks, that almost 1000 hr

Per year lost of distraction. After that, people feel like that there's "not enough time" to achieve their goals. The reality is it's not about lacking of time; it's about lacking of effective time management.

The journey to mastering time management begins with small steps with daily practice. Start by understanding where your time goes and what tasks are truly valuable. Learn to go for perfectionism and focus on progress. Enhance your techniques and set your priorities, and most importantly, approach time as a way to align your daily actions with your biggest dreams and inner purpose.

⁕ In this chapter, I will explore not only practical techniques of time management but also how to align your schedule with your life purpose. You will discover how to sideline distractions, focus on what truly matters, and create balance between work, personal growth, and inner peace.

Why Time Management Matters

Time management is very crucial because time is limited. Everyone has 24 hours in a day. The way we allocate our time affects every area of life, whether it's achieving career success, building stronger relationships, or any type of profession.

Because in today's world, where distractions are in every step, the way to manage your time effectively is more essential than ever. Time management isn't about staying organized or meeting deadlines; it's about maximizing productivity, reducing stress, and aligning your actions with your goals.

At its core, time management empowers you to make deliberate choices about how you spend your time, ensuring that you prioritize what truly matters. Without effective time management, it's easy to feel overwhelmed, scattered, and disconnected from your long-term goals.

One of the key reasons time management matters is its impact on productivity. When you manage your time effectively, you ensure that you are dedicating your attention to highly prioritized tasks that contribute to your overall goals.

Eg: A startup founder struggles to balance investor meetings, product development, and team management.

To stay on top of everything, he adopts the "Theme Day" approach:

Monday: For team meetings & strategy

Wednesday: For product development

Friday: For investor updates & marketing

This unique method ensures focused time for critical areas without mixing priorities, improving productivity & clarity.

Understanding Your Relationship with Time

1. Time as Investment

To truly grasp the concept of time management, we must first shift our mindset—time is not something we spend; it is something we invest. Each hour spent should contribute toward your goals & aspirations, providing value in return.

Ask yourself:

How much value is this activity bringing to my life?

Is this task moving me closer to my goals?

If not, it's time to reconsider how you're allocating your time. The goal is to align your time with what truly matters.

"Your time is limited, so don't waste it living someone else's life." – Steve Jobs

The more intentional you become about how you invest your time, the more rewarding your results will be.

2. Identify Time Drains

Time drains are activities, habits, or behaviors that consume hours without contributing meaningful steps toward your goals. These are often disguised as tasks that may seem urgent but hold little value in the long run.

To take control of your time, you must first become self-aware of these time drains.

Ask yourself:

What tasks consistently pull me away from my goals?

Where am I spending unnecessary hours without making meaningful progress?

The key is to identify these drains and either reduce or eliminate them entirely. By becoming conscious of how you're spending your time, you gain the power to restructure your focus toward what truly matters.

"Time is what we want most, but what we use worst." – William Penn

3. Time Value Mindset – with the 80/20 Rule (Pareto Principle)

The Time Value Mindset is about recognizing that not all tasks hold the same level of importance or return on investment (ROI).

Some tasks contribute significantly toward your goals, while others provide minimal or no real value.

To manage your time more effectively, you need to focus on tasks that yield the most impact rather than wasting time on activities that don't contribute much.

The key idea is like that -

Not all efforts are created equal.

A small percentage of tasks produce the majority of results.

The 80/20 rule (P.P)

The 80/20 rule states that 80% of your results come from 20% of your efforts.

In other words, a small portion of what you do is responsible for the majority of your success, while the rest contribute little.

Let's break this down with an example -

Imagine you have 10 tasks to complete.

2 of those tasks (20%) will likely yield 80% of your results – these are highly impact tasks.

The remaining 8 tasks will contribute 20% of your results – these are lower impact tasks.

Example - Let's say your goal is to increase productivity in your business.

High impact task (20%)

Focus on tasks like developing a new product, networking, or completing critical work projects that drive significant progress.

These will generate the majority of your result, leading to success.

Low impact tasks (80%)

Tasks like replying to emails, attending unnecessary meetings, or spending time on social media.

While these tasks may feel urgent, they contribute far less to your overall goals.

By focusing on the most impactful 20% of your efforts, you maximize your productivity and ensure your time is spent on what truly matters.

"Don't count every hr. in the day, make every hr. count." – Anonymous

4. Personal time rhythms:

Every person has a unique energy pattern throughout the day. Understanding and aligning with your natural rhythm can significantly boost your productivity.
Instead of forcing yourself to work at times when your energy is down, you can plan your tasks to match your energy levels.

Most people experience peak energy levels at specific times of the day. These are your golden hours, when your focus, creativity, and problem-solving abilities are at their highest.

Morning – Ideal for deep work, like strategizing, writing, or tackling complex problems.

Afternoon – Best for tasks that require moderate energy, such as meetings or follow-ups.

Evening – Suitable for light tasks, like reviewing notes or planning the next day.

By working with your natural energy flow, you can accomplish more in less time and feel less exhausted by the end of the day.

Personal time rhythms are not about working harder—they are about working smarter.

During low-energy times, focus and productivity naturally drop. Instead of pushing through, use this time for less demanding tasks, like responding to messages, organizing your workspace, or taking a break.

While it's important to align with your natural rhythm, life isn't always predictable. Each day brings different challenges—adjust when needed, but maintain a general structure.

Work when your brain is at its peak, rest when it's not." – Tim Ferriss

Time Management as a Practice, Not a One-Time Effort

Time management isn't something you master once and never revisit—it's a practice that requires ongoing attention and consistent effort, self-reflection, and adjustment. Just as physical fitness requires regular exercise, managing time effectively demands daily practice.

Every day presents new challenges and demands. What worked yesterday might not work today. Regularly refine your time management strategies based on your current situation and responsibilities.

Life is unpredictable, and a rigid schedule can sometimes cause stress. Adaptability is key to effective time management—adjust your plan as needed without losing focus on your goals.

~ Start your day with a clear plan.
~ Schedule breaks to avoid burnout.
~ End your day by preparing for tomorrow.

By mastering time management as a continuous practice, don't be discouraged by setbacks or days when things don't go as planned.

By treating time management as a continuous practice, you not only become more productive but also develop a deeper understanding of how to balance work, goals, and life. Consistency is the foundation of long-term success.

The "No Zero Day" Philosophy

Have you ever felt stuck, like you didn't make progress toward your goal? That's what people call a "zero day"—a day when you do nothing to move forward. The No Zero Day philosophy is all about making sure every day counts, even in a small way.

The No zero day philosophy is simple but powerful in managing your time and productivity. It enhances the importance of consistency and progress, no matter how small. The term no zero day means making progress toward your goal every single day without letting a day go by where you do nothing.

It's about breaking the habit of doing nothing and replacing it with small, intentional actions that lead to growth. The goal isn't to achieve perfection but to ensure that you are always moving forward, no matter how small the steps may seem.

Why does it work?

1. Building Momentum:

It is the process of creating forward progress in a steady, ongoing way. When you focus on consistent small actions every day, they compound over time and gradually lead to larger achievements. Small actions lead to big results. At first the progress you make feel slow or insignificant.

But those small actions start to accumulate. A small wins create a sense of progress and confidence. At beginning you start to build confidence fuels further action. Leading to positivity and reduce the feeling of overwhelming. Large and complex goals can feel overwhelming and impossible when you focus on the end results. Building momentum allows you to break tasks into manageable chunks. Making progress feel achievable.

Example of Building Momentum:
Business growth—consistently making small improvements, whether it's sending one email, networking, or focusing on completing small tasks that contribute to significant growth.

2. Breaking Procrastination:

It is one of the biggest obstacles to productivity. It's that nagging habit of putting off important tasks and doing less meaningful activities instead. Breaking procrastination isn't about forcing yourself to do everything perfectly. It's about understanding why it happens and developing strategies to overcome it.

Why do people procrastinate?

1. Fear of failure
2. Overwhelm
3. Lack of clarity
4. Instant gratification

How to Break Procrastination:

Start Small: The best way to overcome procrastination is to reduce the size of the task instead of avoiding it completely.
Finish the whole project. Commit to working on it for just 10 min. Once you start, you often find it easier to keep going.

Focus on Next Steps: If tasks feel overwhelming, break it into smaller, actionable steps. Instead of saying "I need to write an essay," focus on writing the introduction or even just brainstorming ideas.

Eliminate Distractions: Identify what pulls your attention away—like your phone, social media, or TV—and create an environment that supports focus. Simple actions like turning off notifications or working in a quiet space can make a big difference.

Let's say you have been procrastinating on sending follow-up emails to potential clients. You keep delaying it, thinking, "I'll do it when I have more time." Instead of waiting, you take one small step today—write and send just one email. Tomorrow, you send another. By the end of the week, you have reached out to 5 clients, and one of them might reply.

This small daily action breaks the procrastination cycle and builds momentum for your business.

The good news about procrastination is it can be broken. By understanding why it happens and taking small, deliberate steps, you can replace procrastination with productive habits and take control of your time.

3. Reduce Perfectionism:

Perfectionism is the tendency to set extremely high standards and feel like anything less than perfect is a failure. While aiming for excellence can be a good thing, perfectionism often leads to procrastination and fear of taking action. It makes a task overwhelming because "nothing even seems good enough."

Reducing perfectionism means shifting your mindset from needing things to be flawless to focusing on progress and growth. It's about recognizing that small, imperfect actions are better than doing nothing at all.

Reducing perfectionism matters because it:

1. Overcomes fear of starting
2. Encourages progress
3. Builds confidence

Example : Let's say you were writing a business pitch, but you keep rewriting the introduction, hoping to make it perfect. Days go by. If you're stuck instead of aiming for flawless, you decide to write a rough draft first. It's not perfect, but it's a start. Point is, later you can refine it. This shift helps you finish the pitch faster & reduces the pressure to get it right on the first try.

Scheduling downtime

In the pursuit of goals, it's easy to believe that constant effort and endless work are the only path to success. However, this type of mindset to exhaustion, stress, and diminishing viewpoint. While hard work is essential, rest is equally important. This is where scheduling downtime comes into play.

Downtime isn't about wasting time or being unproductive. It's a strategic technique to recharge yourself—mind, body, and focus. Think of something different, like sharpening the axe before chopping wood. It makes the process more efficient and less draining. In fact, some of the most successful people intentionally schedule breaks into their daily routines, knowing that rest enhances their focus, creativity, and decision-making abilities.

Downtime plays a crucial role in improving both productivity and well-being. Here's why:

1. Prevents Burnout
2. Boosts Creativity
3. Improves Focus & Decision Making
4. Enhances Relationships

1) Prevent Burnout:

Continuous work burnout is a state of physical, emotional, and mental exhaustion caused by excessive work and stress. It occurs when we push ourselves too hard without taking necessary time to rest and recover.

In today's fast-paced world, where productivity is often prioritized, burnout has become a common concern, especially for those who have multiple responsibilities in both their personal and professional lives.

Burnout doesn't happen overnight; it's the result of sustained stress and a lack of balance between work and rest.

Signs of Burnout:

Feeling emotionally drained and disconnected from tasks.

A decrease in motivation and productivity.

Increased feelings of frustration, anxiety, or irritability.

Physical symptoms such as fatigue, headaches, and trouble sleeping.

When you don't take regular breaks, your energy becomes depleted, and your ability to perform at your best diminishes. Burnout can lead to long-term damage to both your mental health and productivity. Preventing burnout is not about avoiding work but rather about balancing efforts with rest. Downtime is a powerful tool that allows you to maintain productivity without sacrificing your well-being. By prioritizing regular breaks,

Let's say you are working long hours on projects without taking breaks. Over time, you feel drained, your productivity decreases, and you start making careless mistakes. By scheduling regular downtime or simply disconnecting from your work for a few minutes, you restore your energy and maintain your mental health and physical health.

2) Boost Creativity:

Creativity isn't something that can be forced; it flourishes when we step away from constant work and give our minds the freedom to roam. Many people believe that more work equals more ideas, but research shows that long hours of relentless effort often lead to burnout rather than big breakthroughs. Creativity increases when we allow ourselves time to relax, reflect, and explore.

When we are constantly busy, our minds areOverload with tasks, deadlines, and distractions. This mental clutter reduces our ability to think creatively. Creativity isn't just about coming up with new ideas; it's about solving problems in innovative ways. Downtime allows you to step back from challenges, giving you more energy & the space to approach problems from different perspectives. When your mind is rested and less stressed, you're more likely to view issues as opportunities leading to more effective & creative solutions.

Imagine you're struggling to come up with a solution for a complex business problem. You have spent long hours trying to find solutions, but nothing seems to click. By stepping away, taking a break, or engaging in a creative activity like writing or walking, your brain begins to make connections in the background. Suddenly, a fresh idea or new approaches emerge. This is the power of allowing your mind the space to reset & recharge.

Creativity isn't about hard work; it's about smart work. Downtime provides the mental space necessary for your brain to relax, reflect, and generate new ideas. By embracing rest, you are not slowing your progress; you are fueling your brain and enhancing overall productivity.

3) Improve focus and decision-making:

Effective time management relies heavily on two key skills: focus and decision-making. These abilities are interconnected.and play a vital role in helping you achieve your goals, reduce stress, and use your time wisely.

Focus is the ability to set a direction of your mental energy towards a specific task without distraction. In a world full of interruptions, mastering focus is essential for productivity. It helps you enhance your efficiency.

When you focus on one task at a time, you complete it faster and with higher quality.

It helps you reduce stress. A clear focus helps you feel in control of your time, reducing the overwhelm that comes from many tasks.

It enhances your strengths in discipline. Staying focused trains your brain to resist distractions, making it easier to stay consistent.

Decision-making is about choosing how to prioritize your time, energy, and tasks. Strong decision-making ensures that your focus & direction are aligned with the activities that matter most.

It helps you prevent wasting time. Poor decisions lead to wasted time on unimportant tasks.

It enhances your clarity, which leads to clear decisions and eliminates confusion about what to do next.

Making decisions quickly and confidently empowers your actions and builds momentum.

Example: Imagine you are working on launching a product without focus. You might try to juggle marketing, product design, and customer communication all at once. However, with clear decision-making, you prioritize one task, finalize the design, and focus exclusively on it.

This ensures high quality output and steady progress.

Focus and decision-making are the pillars of effective time management. Together, they help you avoid distractions, prioritize what truly matters, and achieve your goals efficiently. Mastering these skills will not only improve your productivity but also bring greater clarity and confidence to your daily routine.

Insights on Time Management

Time management is often seen as a purely practical skill, involving schedules, deadlines, and productivity tools. However, approached from a spiritual perspective, it takes on a deeper meaning. Time becomes more than just hours and minutes—it becomes a gift, a resource to align your actions with your higher purpose and inner peace.

Staying present in the moment:
Mindfulness teaches us to be fully present in whatever task we are doing, instead of being consumed by regrets of the past or worries about the future. When you are mindful, you:

Work with greater focus & clarity.
Reduce distractions, leading to better productivity.
Experience a sense of peace, even during busy moments.

Example: Starting your day with 5-10 min of meditation can help ground you, allowing you to approach tasks with calmness and intention.

Gratitude

Every second of life is a gift, and practicing gratitude for time helps us value it more deeply. Instead of wasting time on trivial matters or procrastination, gratitude reminds us to use each moment wisely.

Reflect at the end of the day: What did I do today that was meaningful?

Celebrate small wins and progress, no matter how minor they seem.

Gratitude shifts your mindset from seeing time as a burden to viewing it as an opportunity for growth and connection.

Not everything in life can be planned or controlled, and that's okay. Spiritual insights remind us to trust the process and allow life to flow naturally. This doesn't mean neglecting responsibilities but understanding that some delays or changes can lead to better opportunities. Instead of rushing through life, spiritual practices encourage slowing down to appreciate the journey.

Whether it's through prayer, meditation, or simply quiet time, these moments of stillness help you recharge and reconnect with yourself. Spiritual time isn't about being efficient—it's about being intentional.

By practicing mindfulness, gratitude, and aligning your time with your values, you create a life that is not only productive but also meaningful and fulfilling.

------------------ **chapter summary**------------------

- Time is more than productivity – Effective time management creates balance, purpose, and fulfillment in life.
- Combining strategies like the No Zero Day philosophy with spiritual insights enhances effectiveness.
- Time is not a one-time effort but a lifelong skill that requires regular and consistent practice.
- Small actions create a big impact – Small and consistent actions each day can create a big impact.
- The No Zero Day philosophy showed us the power of small and daily efforts, proving that consistency is more important than perfection.
- Live with purpose – Use time as a gift to create a life filled with success and inner peace.

III

Bond of Relationship

In the journey of success, no one achieves greatness alone. Behind every accomplished individual is a network of mentors who guide, peers who collaborate, and supporters who uplift. Building and nurturing meaningful relationships is not just a skill; it is an essential pillar of growth, both in business and life.

Networking is not about collecting contacts; it's about building meaningful connections that create useful value. In today's world, a strong network can open doors to opportunities that hard work alone might not achieve. But it's not just about professional relationships. Deep, genuine connections with others also fuel personal growth, provide emotional strength, and enrich your life. At the same time, strong relationships are more than professional assets. They form the foundation of trust, collaboration, and emotional well-being, whether in business or your personal life.

Learning how to connect meaningfully with others helps you succeed while staying grounded while you chase your dreams. Success is not just about achieving goals; it is about helping people and making a difference in the lives of others, creating value for them.

This chapter will explore the art of networking and relationship-building, providing practical insights into how to grow and maintain a strong network. You'll learn how to connect with others authentically, build trust, and create meaningful partnerships that align with your values and goals. We'll also touch on the spiritual dimension of relationships—how forming genuine connections can bring you closer to your purpose and inner peace.

Success becomes far more fulfilling when it's shared. Whether it's a mentor who helps you overcome obstacles, a partner who collaborates on a business idea, or a friend who motivates you to keep going, relationships are the key to unlocking your full potential. Networking and relationships are not just tools for success; they are the essence of a rich, purposeful, and rewarding life.

How Connections Shape Success

Success is never a solo energy. Behind every remarkable achievement lies a network of people who supported, guided, or collaborated to make it happen. Connections have the power to transform your path, offering opportunities, insights, and strength in ways you might not achieve alone.

First connections open doors to opportunities. Think about it—many of life's biggest breakthroughs happen because someone believed in you and extended a helping hand, whether it's a mentor recommending you for a job, a colleague introducing you to a potential client, or a friend sharing a valuable resource, the right Connection can change everything. These aren't mere coincidences; they're the result of nurturing meaningful relationships.

Beyond opportunities, connections bring knowledge and expertise. When you're surrounded by people with diverse experiences, you gain access to insights you might not discover on your own. A mentor might share a strategy that saves you years of trial and error. They might offer feedback that sharpens your ideas. Your network becomes a pool of wisdom that accelerates your growth.

But relationships aren't just about professional gains; they also provide emotional support. Success is rarely a straight road, and there will be moments when doubt creeps in or obstacles feel overwhelming. During these times, having someone to encourage you, offer perspective, or simply listen can make all the difference. A strong connection can reignite your motivation and remind you of your potential.

Connections also enhance your credibility and influence. When someone respected in your field vouches for you, it builds trust with others. A recommendation or endorsement from the right person can open doors that hard work alone might not unlock. This ripple effect of relationships often leads to even more connections, creating a cycle of growth and success.

Example:

Imagine a freelance graphic designer, Alex, who meets a startup founder at a local event. The founder hires Alex for small projects. Impressed by Alex's work, the founder recommends him to others. Over time, Alex's client base grows significantly—all because of one meaningful connection.

Ultimately, connections shape success because they remind us that we're stronger together. They're not just about advancing your goals; they're about building a life enriched by shared experiences, mutual growth, and meaningful bonds. By investing in genuine relationships, you're investing in a foundation for lasting success—both professionally and personally.

The Ripple Effect of Networking

The ripple effect of networking shows how one meaningful connection can lead to a series of opportunities, relationships, and achievements. It's the process where a single interaction creates a chain reaction, extending far beyond the initial point of contact.

Every time you build a relationship, you aren't just connecting with one person—you're tapping into their network as well. This interconnectedness creates an expanding web of potential opportunities. Think of it like Throwing a stone into a calm lake—the ripples grow outward, affecting areas far beyond the initial splash. This is the mechanism of the ripple effect.

Example:

Consider a young entrepreneur who meets an investor at a conference. The investor not only funds their startup but also introduces them to experienced mentors and potential clients. These new connections lead to partnerships, collaborations, and even more growth. What started as one connection cascades into a network of opportunities.

Why It's Powerful:

The ripple effect of networking is powerful because it amplifies opportunities, expands influence, and accelerates growth in ways that would be impossible alone. Here's why:

1. Exponential Growth:

A single connection can introduce you to multiple opportunities, creating a multiplying effect.

Each new relationship leads to further introductions, creating a vast web of possibilities over time.

2. Unexpected Benefits:

Opportunities often come from people or connections you least expect.

For example, a casual conversation at an event might lead to a major business deal or career opportunity.

3. Credibility and Trust:

When someone in your network vouches for you, it builds trust with others.

A personal recommendation carries weight, making others more willing to work with or support you.

4. Access to Resources:

The ripple effect connects you with people who have skills, knowledge, or resources you may not have.

It bridges gaps, helping you overcome challenges more efficiently.

5. Momentum for Success:

The ripple effect creates momentum, where one opportunity leads to another, accelerating your journey toward your goals.

It's a chain reaction that grows stronger as your network expands.

The Role of Authenticity

The ripple effect works best when your connections are genuine, building authentic relationships based on trust, mutual respect, and shared values.

This creates a strong foundation for opportunities to flourish. It's not about networking for personal gain but about creating value for others as well.

The ripple effect of networking highlights the importance of even small connections—one genuine interaction can trigger a series of events that lead to opportunities far beyond your imagination. By nurturing relationships and staying open to possibilities, you're not just building a network—you're creating waves that carry you toward success.

Heartbeat of Relationships

Relationships are the foundation of both personal and professional success. But what makes a relationship strong and lasting? It's not about frequent interactions or shared goals—it's about the core qualities that give a relationship life and depth.

The heartbeat of a relationship refers to the essential elements: trust, authenticity, empathy, and mutual respect that keep connections meaningful and alive. Just like a healthy heartbeat sustains life, these qualities sustain relationships. Without them, even the strongest connections can weaken over time.Looking bonds can weaken over time.

So, this topic will explore how these fundamental traits shape relationships, why they are important, and how they can elevate your personal and professional connections. By understanding and embracing them, you not only achieve success but also bring genuine value to your life.

In strong relationships, there are a few core elements that make them meaningful and lasting. Let's break them down clearly:

1) TRUST: CORE OF CONNECTION

Trust is the heart of any meaningful relationship. Without it, even frequent interactions or shared goals can feel shallow. It's what allows people to rely on you, share openly, and build lasting connections.

Without trust, even frequent interactions lose their depth, and relationships become fragile. On the other hand, when trust is present, it opens the door to collaboration, understanding, and shared success.

Trust is essential. It shapes relationships, and simple ways to build & strengthen it. Understanding trust isn't just about improving relationships—it's about creating a solid foundation for long-term success in all areas of life.

_ To Build Trust:

1. Be honest – Always tell the truth, even if it's not easy.

1) Keep Your Promises - Do what you say you will.

2) Stay Consistent - Regularly show through your actions that you're reliable and genuine.

Power of Trust

Imagine you're working on a project. If your team trusts you, they'll listen to your ideas, support your decisions, and go the extra mile for you. Trust creates a ripple effect, spreading positivity and strengthening bonds.

Building trust takes time, but it's worth every effort. When you earn someone's trust, you gain more than just a connection—you gain a foundation for mutual growth and success.

2) Authenticity: Be Genuine

Authenticity is the foundation of meaningful connections. It's about being genuine—showing your true self rather than putting on a mask. It's the quality that makes people trust and respect you because they know you're not pretending or trying to fit into someone else's mold.

Authenticity allows relationships to thrive because they're built on honesty, not pretense.

When you're authentic, you attract people who resonate with your values, creating deeper, more honest relationships. Pretending to be someone you're not might bring short-term gains, but genuine connections lead to long-term trust and success.

To Be Authentic:

1. Know Your Values – Understand what matters most to you and let your actions reflect those principles.

2. Speak Honestly – Share your thoughts and feelings openly, even if they're not perfect. People appreciate honesty over perfection.

3. Accept Imperfections – Nobody is perfect, and that's okay. Embrace your flaws—they make you human and relatable.

The Impact of Authenticity

When you're authentic, you create relationships that are real and lasting. For example, a business leader who openly shares their challenges earns more respect than one who pretends to have all the answers.

By being true to yourself, you allow others to do the same, creating an environment where connections are honest, supportive, and enduring. Authenticity isn't just about relationships; it's a way of living that leads to genuine success.

3) Empathy: Understand and Care

Empathy is the ability to understand and share the feelings of others. It's what allows you to connect on a deeper level, making people feel seen, heard, and valued.

In relationships, empathy builds trust, strengthens bonds, and fosters mutual understanding

In a fast-paced world, empathy helps build trust and strengthen bonds by showing others that their emotions and perspectives matter. It's the bridge that connects people on a deeper level. Fostering relationships that are both supportive and enduring, empathy is essential. It enhances communication, and by practicing it, we can transform both personal and professional relationships.

How to Practice Empathy

1. Listen Actively – Pay full attention when someone is speaking. Avoid interrupting or forming a response in your head while they talk.

2. Ask Questions – Show interest in their feelings by asking thoughtful questions like, "How did that make you feel?"

3. Put Yourself in Their Shoes – Imagine how you would feel in their situation to better understand their perspective.

The Power of Empathy

Empathy can turn a casual acquaintance into a trusted ally. For example, a manager who listens and acknowledges an employee's challenges fosters loyalty and trust. Similarly, in personal relationships, understanding and validating feelings can resolve conflicts and deepen connections.

Empathy is not just a skill; it's a mindset of compassion and understanding. By practicing empathy, you create relationships that are supportive, meaningful, and resilient.

4. Mutual Respect

Mutual respect is about valuing each other's opinions, boundaries, and contributions. It's a two-way street where both parties feel seen, heard, and appreciated.

When respect is present, relationships thrive because there is a sense of equality and fairness. Mutual respect is the cornerstone of strong and healthy relationships, which are essential for success. It ensures that every interaction is built on equality and understanding.

How to Cultivate Mutual Respect

1. Listen Actively – Pay attention to what others say without interrupting or dismissing their views.

2. Acknowledge Contributions – Show appreciation for others' efforts, even in small ways.

3. Set Boundaries – Respect others' personal and professional limits and expect the same in return.

The Ripple Effect of Respect

Mutual respect doesn't just enhance one-on-one relationships; it creates a positive environment where everyone feels valued.

For example, a manager who respects their team earns loyalty and motivates higher performance. When mutual respect is the foundation of your relationships, they become healthier, more productive, and enduring.

It's a simple yet powerful way to create meaningful connections that benefit everyone involved.

The Heartbeat of Relationships . The core elements of relationships lie in trust, authenticity empathy, and mutual respect. These qualities form the foundation for meaningful and lasting connections. When nurtured, they create relationships that are not only supportive but also crucial for personal and professional success.

By prioritizing these values, we can build bonds that thrive and stand the test of time.

The Circle of Value

In any relationship, whether personal or professional, creating value isn't a one-way process. The Circle of Value is a powerful concept that emphasizes the importance of mutual contribution. It's about understanding that both parties need to give and receive value for the relationship to truly thrive.

When we focus on providing value to others—whether through time, knowledge, or resources—we build trust, deepen connections, and create a foundation for long-term success.

Why It Matters

1. Mutual Contribution Builds Trust

In the Circle of Value, relationships thrive when we offer value without expecting something in return.

This builds trust, as people feel valued and appreciated, creating stronger bonds.

2. Long-Term Growth and Success

Relationships built on mutual value are more sustainable.

Both parties grow together, fostering collaboration and shared success.

Instead of one-sided interactions, the Circle of Value ensures everyone contributes to each other's goals, leading to long-term prosperity.

3. Win-Win Outcomes

Focusing on adding value to others creates a dynamic where both sides benefit. This leads to deeper connections, stronger networks, and more opportunities for growth and success.

The Circle of Value highlights the importance of mutual giving and receiving in building strong relationships. By offering knowledge, time, or resources, trust is created, bonds are strengthened, and long-term success is fostered.

When both parties contribute, relationships grow naturally, leading to shared growth and win-win outcomes. Moving beyond one-sided interactions, we create meaningful connections that benefit everyone involved.

Embracing this concept lays the foundation for deeper relationships and greater opportunities and lasting success.

The Art of Networking

Networking isn't about exchanging business cards or collecting contacts—it's about building meaningful relationships that create mutual value and long-term success.

In today's fast-paced, interconnected world, networking goes beyond attending events. It's about creating authentic connections that add value to both parties.

The art of networking focuses on offering your expertise, building trust, and maintaining relationships over time—whether in person or through digital platforms like LinkedIn and social media. Effective networking helps you tap into new opportunities, expand your influence, and grow both personally and professionally.

1. Building Genuine Connections

At its core, networking is about forming authentic relationships built on trust and shared interests. Instead of seeking quick gains, focus on providing value to others—whether through your expertise, knowledge, or resources. When you contribute to others' growth, you build stronger bonds that last.

2. Offer Value and Support

Networking isn't just about what you can take but what you can give . By offering your skills, insights or support. You help other succed and they are More likely to support you in return. In today's digital world plateform like linkedin and social media make it eaiser to connect and provide value across wide network.

3. Consistency and Digital Networking

In today's digital age, maintaining relationships online is just as important as in-person networking. Regularly engage with your network through messages, comments, and shared content. Digital tools allow you to stay connected, offer value, and expand your reach.

By mastering the art of networking, you will build lasting relationships that foster growth, provide opportunities, and lead to mutual success—both online and offline.

Spiritual Insights: Network & Relationships

Relationships built on spiritual principles like trust, empathy, and authenticity transcend mere transactions. They become a source of mutual growth and purpose. Networking isn't just about gaining contacts; it's about creating meaningful connections that aligns with your values and help you in grow personally and professionally.

When you show up as your true self without pretense or hidden agendas. You attract people who resonate with your energy. In spritual networking the Focus is on giving not just taking when you offer your support expertise or kindness without expecting immediate return, you create a ripple effect of goodwill.

-------------Chapter summary----------------

· Strong authentic connection are the cornerstone of success

· Trust , empathy and genuine relationship drive growth and opportunities

· The circle of value emphasizes the importance of giving and receiving value for mutual growth.

· Quality connection are the More impactful than the number of networks

· Spritual alignment such as empathy and puspose elevates networking

· Building authentic relationship open door to long term success.

IV
The leadership

In world of entrepreneurship success is rarely comes from individual effort alone. The leader who understand the power of bringing people together, align their strength and working towards a common goal that truly thrive " lead to unite" explore the art of leadership how visionary leaders Foster collaboration, inspire team and crate a sinse of unite . True leadership don't just manage they unite.

Great leadership are not just those who give orders but those who build connection, empower others and foster an environment where everyone feels value and motivated. True leadership is about bringing diverse individual togather, encouraging them to work as one.

Whether you're guiding a team, building a business or striving for meaningful impact. " Lead to unite " will show you how to lead with purpose empathy and vision that inspire others to follow. Let's unlock the power of leadership that unites and transform.

Spark of leadership

Leadership isn't about title authority, or position it starts with a spark. The Spark is the energy that sets a leader Apart , igniting passion and purpose within themselves and others. It is the invisible force that inspire people to believe, act unite around a Shared vision.

At it's core the Spark of leadership begins with clarity. Great leaders have the ability to see beyond the present, envisioning a future that other may not yet imagine. But Vision alone isn't enough. Its the courage to act , to take that first step into the unknown that, truly light the flame of leadership.

Leadership requires courage the courage to act when the future is uncertain to take that first step,even when the road ahead is unknown. It's what enables a leader to take responsibility. Make tough desecion and keep moving forward when faced challenges.
However, the Spark of leadership doesn't just come from personal drive; it's fueled by empathy. A leader must connect with others, understanding their struggles and aspirations. This connection build trust and loyalty, creating a bond that inspire others to follow.
Empathy builds trust, and trust is the foundation of any successful team . True leadership is not About commanding from distance but about walking alongside other, lifting them up , and inspiring them to reach their potential.
A great leader also demonstrate integrity. Leadership without honesty and strong moral principles is shallow and unsuitable. Integrity ensures that Leaders words align with their actions. It builds credibility and earn respect which are essential for inspiring trust and loyalty in others.
Adaptability is another vital quality of leader. Challenges are unexpected situations often arise and leaders must remain flexible and open mind adaptability allows them to think creativity pivot.

When unnecessary, and find solutions even in the face of uncertainty.

Finally, leadership isn't about the ideas and felling it about action. A vision without action is a merely a dream. Great leaderds turn their ideas into reality through determination and costient effort . They lead by an example, showing their team what is possible action create momentum and, momentum inspire other to step up and contribute. It's through action that leaders spark spreads lighting a fire in those around them.

Consider the story of elon musk , who envisoned a whole world by sustainable energy. This spark of leadership lead to tesla and space X companies that disrupted Industries and inspired millions, musk's courage to take risks and his relentless action turned his vision in golabal reality.

This Spark of leadership is not sometimes extraordinary or unttainable , it starts with small steps a thought, an idea or decision. It grows courage empathy and action. Leadership isn't about perfection or power. Its about igniting the Spark within yourself and inspiring others . The journey may not always be easy, but every great leader starts the same way with a single spark. Are you ready to ignite yours ?

The science of Synergy

The term "Synergy" originates from the Greek word Synergos, meaning "working together." In scientific contexts, synergy often refers to interactions between components that produce an enhanced outcome. Synergy is more than just working together; it's the magic that happens when a group of individuals combines their strengths, skills, and efforts to create results greater than what they could achieve alone.

Synergy transforms simple coordination into powerful for success. Think of Synergy as 1+1 =3 . It is the idea that the whole is greater than the sum of its parts. While coordination ensure tasks are completed smoothly. Synergy takes this further by amplifying the impact of combined efforts. Synergy isn't just a concept; it's a science rooted in human psychology, group dynamics and effective leadership. When people align their efforts, skills and energy towards a common goal.

Building Block of Synergy.

1. Alignment of Goals

The first step in creating synergy is ensuring everyone is moving in the same direction. A shared vision acts as the glue that binds a team together, connecting their efforts toward a common purpose. Example: A rowing team paddling in sync moves faster and smoother than one out of rhythm.

2. Combining Diverse Strengths

Each person brings unique skills to the table. By combining these strengths, teams innovate and solve problems effectively.

Example A tech startup thrives because the programer builds the marketer sells and the startegies plans.

3. Trust and Communication

For synergy to flourish, team members must trust each other and communicate openly. Trust fosters collaboration, while effective communication ensures ideas flow freely and tasks are coordinated efficiently.

Example: A family planning a wedding succeeds through clear roles and honest discussions, avoiding chaos.

Science of 1 + 1 = 3

When two individuals combine their efforts, the overlap of their skills, ideas, and energy produces a new dynamic. Their collective output exceeds the simple addition of their individual contributions.

Synergy is more than coordination—it's the magic that happens when people work together with trust, purpose, and alignment. It's the difference between a group of individuals and a unified team.

When you understand and apply the science of synergy, you unlock the power to achieve extraordinary results. So, ask yourself: Are you building synergy in your team? If not, it's time to ignite the spark. Because in the science of synergy,
1 + 1 truly equals 3.

Leadership Under Pressure

Leadership isn't about sailing when everything is perfect; it's about guiding your team when challenges arise. True leaders thrive under pressure, using obstacles as opportunities to inspire, adapt, and succeed. When heat is on, a leader's strength, clarity, and ability to stay composed define their impact. Pressure doesn't just test a leader—it shapes them.

Think of a captain steering a ship. In calm waters, anyone can hold the wheel. But when the waves rise, and the storm hits, it takes a steady hand, quick thinking, and unshakable resolve to bring the crew safely to shore. That's what leadership under pressure is all about.

Key Qualities of a Leader Under Pressure

1. Stay Calm, Stay Focused

When pressure strikes, the leader's reaction sets the tone. Staying calm isn't a choice; it's a strategy. A calm mind thinks clearly, makes better decisions, and inspires confidence in others. When a leader remains calm, it creates a ripple effect throughout the team. People start to believe that if their leader can handle the situation, they can too.

Calmness is contagious—it sets the tone and helps the team focus on solutions instead of problems.

Staying focused under pressure is equally crucial. It's about directing your energy toward solutions, not problems. Staying focused allows a leader to prioritize and tackle the most critical tasks. Instead of getting lost in the noise of crisis, a focused leader channels their energy toward actionable steps. This focus is what transforms pressure into progress.

Quick Tips to Lead with Calm and Focus:

1.Take a Breath: A pause helps you regain clarity.

2. Simplify: Focus on the most critical tasks.

3. Lead by Example: Your calmness will inspire others.

Remember: Calmness gives you clarity. Focus gives you direction. Together, they make you unstoppable even under great pressure.

2. Discipline

Those who master discipline in life become true kings. Discipline is what sets a king apart from a servant. A job is for those who need others to impose discipline on them, while a king is self-disciplined, driven by his own sense of purpose. For instance servent rushes to the office by 8. AM . Out of fear that the boss might already be there , but a king shows up on time because of his commitment not fear.

Discipline can't be taught it is an royal instinct, a royal quality that not everyone process. There is a significant differences between a job and profession . A job merely a layer under profession. Not everyone can thrive in a profession because success demands certain qualities and one of the most essential thing is discipline and hardwork togather are the foundation of true leadership.

Quick techniques to lead with discipline:

1. Set clear goals: to stay focused on priorities.

2. Create a daily routine: to build costient habits

3. Track progress: to stay motivated and adjust strategies.

Remember: Discipline turn goal into achivement.

3. Quick Decision Making

The ability to make quick and effective decisions is a crucial skill. Leaders often face situations where there's no time to deliberate extensively, and hesitation can lead to missed opportunities. Quick decision-making is not about rushing, but rather having the confidence, clarity,and ability to act decisively when necessary. It's about making the right choice fast.

Effective leaders know that every decision counts, whether it's navigating a crisis or seizing an opportunity.

Quick desecion aren't always perfect,but they show a Leader's ability to stay calm. Take calculative risks and guide their team through uncertainty. The power of a leader lies in making the right decision quickly and turning challenges into opportunities.

Techniques to make quick confident desecion.

1. Trust your instincts: rely on your experience to guide you quickly.

2. Simplify the problem: focus only the key factors that matters.

3. Sets the time : limit your desecion making time to avoid overthinking.

I don't believe in taking right desecion, I take desecion and make them Right. ~ Ratan Tata

4. Adaptability

In today's fast-paced world, change is the only constant. Whether it's new technology, shifting market trends, or unexpected challenges, leaders must be ready to adapt quickly. Adaptability is not just about reacting to change; it's about Embracing it, learning from it, and turning it into an advantage.

Think about how businesses had to adjust during the global pandemic. Companies that adapted to remote work, shifted their strategies, or embraced digital transformation thrived, while those who resisted struggled. The same is true for leaders. The ability to stay flexible and open-minded is no longer optional; it's essential. Adaptability is what separates great leaders from the rest. Those who accept change, stay flexible, and find solutions in challenges will always stay ahead.

How to Be an Adaptable Leader Today:

Stay Curious: Keep learning and exploring new ideas.

Be Flexible: Adjust strategies as situations evolve.

Accept Change: View change as an opportunity to grow.

"The measure of intelligence is the ability to adapt to change."
— Albert Einstein

Inner Insights:

In leadership, true strength comes from within. Spiritual insights help leaders stay grounded, act with integrity, and make decisions that align with their deeper values. It's not about following rules but about leading with authenticity, creating an environment of trust, and inspiring teams through purpose.

Spiritual leaders know that success isn't about numbers – it's about making a difference. A great leader leads with a heart, not just a strategy, and that's what creates lasting loyalty. When a leader is driven by purpose, they inspire others to work towards something meaningful.

Integrity is the cornerstone of leadership. A spiritually aware leader makes decisions with fairness and honesty even when no one is watching. This leads to trust, respect, and positive impact, creating an environment where people not only work hard but also feel valued.

------Chapter Summary------

- Unite builds strength; leadership isn't just about guiding—it's about uniting people towards a shared goal.
- Great leadership is tested in tough times; staying calm and decisive is key. Handle pressure with grace.
- The best leaders balance logic with empathy, making decisions that benefit all. See and lead with heart and mind.
- True leadership isn't about success; it's about integrity, wisdom, and higher purpose.
- A leader without purpose is directionless. Strong leadership is driven by vision and values.

V
Whispers of peace

Every one of us is born with a unique power, a force that can drive us to achieve the extraordinary. Inside you lies a power so strong, it's ready to break through any barrier standing in your way. Too often, we let doubt & fear hide this strength, thinking we're not capable of more. But what if the only thing stopping you is the belief that you can't? What if the key to unlocking your greatest success was already within you, waiting to be discovered?

This chapter is your invitation to tap into that power. It's the spark that lights the path toward everything you've ever dreamed of. You don't need to search for strength elsewhere - it's been inside you all along, just waiting for you to recognize it. When you choose to believe in yourself, you'll be amazed at the incredible things you can achieve.

Now is the moment to embrace that inner power. To stop holding back and start believing in what you're truly capable of. It's time to unlock your potential, break through the limits you've set, and step into a future filled with endless possibilities. Your journey to success begins now.

Discovering your potential

The Bhagavad Gita reveals a timeless truth You are far more capable than you believe. Your potential is limitless, waiting to be unleashed, yet often buried beneath doubts, fears, and comparisons.

Krishna's words in the Gita are not just teachings but a call to action, urging you to awaken the immense power already within you.

In Chapter 2, Verse 47, Krishna reminds us:

"Karmanye vadhikaraste ma phaleshu kadachana"

"You have a right to perform your duties, but not to the fruits of your actions."

This profound wisdom tells us to focus on giving our best effort without worrying about the outcome. Many people hold back because they fear failure or crave instant success. But the truth is, success isn't about the destination; it's about committing wholeheartedly to the journey. When you channel your energy into efforts, you unlock the doors to growth and possibilities.

Krishna also speaks of Swadharma—your unique purpose—in Chapter 3. He teaches us that every individual has a special role in this world, a purpose only they can fulfill. But too often, we waste time comparing ourselves to others, doubting our worth, and questioning our abilities. This is where we go wrong.

The path to discovering your potential begins with self-acceptance. Stop measuring yourself by someone else's success. Your strength lies in accepting your journey.

Discovering your potential is not a one-time event, it's a process. Every time you challenge yourself, every time you step out of your comfort zone, you grow closer to unlocking your true strength. Remember your worth is not defined by success or failure but by the courage to keep trying.

The Gita assures us that no action goes to waste, no effort is ever lost. With faith in yourself and the teachings of the Gita, you can break free from limits and achieve what you once thought impossible. Trust yourself, take the leap, and discover the incredible power that's been within you all along.

The Magic of Self-Belief

Self-belief is the foundation of every great success. Without it, even the strongest skills and talents remain unused. The Bhagavad Gita teaches us the power of trusting ourselves. In chapter 6, verse 5, Krishna says:

"Lift yourself with your own mind, don't let your mind pull you down."

The simple yet powerful message reminds us that our thoughts shape our reality. If you think you're capable, you'll find ways to succeed. But if you doubt yourself, you'll create excuses and barriers. The journey of self-belief begins in your mind—it's where every victory starts.

a one-time event, it's a process. Every time you challenge yourself, every time you step out of your comfort zone, you grow closer to unlocking your true strength. Remember your worth is not defined by success or failure but by the courage to keep trying.

The Gita assures us that no action goes to waste, no effort is ever lost. With faith in yourself and the teachings of the Gita, you can break free from limits and achieve what you once thought impossible. Trust yourself, take the leap, and discover the incredible power that's been within you all along.

Think about it: How often have you hesitated to chase a dream because of fear or uncertainty? Maybe you thought, "What if I fail?" or "What if I'm not good enough?" These doubts are normal, but they aren't true. The Gita teaches us that every person carries divine strength within them. You are not ordinary—you are made for greatness.

When you believe in yourself, something magical happens. Your fears lose their grip, and your confidence grows as you start seeing challenges as opportunities to grow, not as reasons to quit. Even if the road ahead seems difficult, self-belief gives you the courage to take the first step. And once you take the step, momentum builds and success becomes inevitable.

Some techniques for self-belief:

Daily consistency: Build your dreams one disciplined step at a time.

Master your time: Control your day, and your goals will follow.

Unshakable focus: Let your determination silence all distractions.

Powerful routine: Craft a daily rhythm that aligns with your success.

Self-belief doesn't mean you'll never face challenges. In fact, life will test you. But the Bhagavad Gita reminds us that these tests are not meant to break you—they are meant to Reveal your strength. Every time you overcome a setback, your belief in yourself becomes stronger.

The spiritual connection to self-belief is simple yet profound—you are not alone in your journey. The divine energy of the universe supports those who trust themselves and take action. Krishna assures us that when we align with our inner power, everything else falls into place.

So, how do you build self-belief? Start by silencing your inner critic. Speak words of encouragement to yourself. Surround yourself with people who uplift you. Most importantly, take small steps every day that remind you of your capabilities. The more you trust yourself, the more you'll achieve.

Remember, your potential is limitless, and your journey begins with a single thought: I can do this. With self-belief, there's no limit to what you can achieve.

Practical Steps to Awaken Power:

There is a limitless strength within you, waiting to be unleashed. It's not something you need to search for—it's already inside you. The key to unlocking it is believing in yourself and taking the first step toward becoming the person you're meant to be.

Imagine waking up every day with energy and excitement, ready to tackle anything that comes your way. Picture yourself achieving your dreams even when obstacles show up. This isn't fantasy—it's your reality waiting to unfold. The power to create this life is already within you, it just needs to be awakened.

The first step to awakening your power is self-reflection. Take a few moments each day to pause and understand who you really are. What are your strengths? What do you truly want out of life? When you know yourself, you can begin making choices that align with your dreams. The more you understand your purpose, the easier it becomes to take action.

Next, focus on positive affirmations. The words you tell yourself matter more than you think. Every day, remind yourself that you are capable. You are strong, and you are worthy of success. These small words can change the way you think and feel, creating a powerful mindset that drives you forward.

Now, you need discipline. Dreams don't become reality overnight—you have to work for them. Set up a daily routine that helps you move toward your goals. It doesn't have to be huge steps every day, but small, consistent actions will add up. Keep going even when it gets tough. This daily effort will build your success, one step at a time.

Lastly, surround yourself with positive people. The right company can inspire you, lift you up, and help you stay focused. Remove negativity from your life, whether it's from others or from your own thoughts. Build a support system that believes in you and your dreams.

The most important step is to take action. Don't wait for a "perfect moment." The time to start is now! Each small action you take brings you closer to the person you want to become. You already have the strength inside you. Trust yourself, step forward, and watch as your power begins to unfold.

The world is waiting for you to step into your greatness.

------------------ **Chapter Summary**--------------------

- True peace comes from within , not external circumstances.
- When action matches your core values , peace naturally follows.
- Daily practice like mediation and self awarness strength your inner peace.
- Trust yourself for it will lead you to life of growth and limitless potential.

VI
The Eternal Guide

In life, we often feel like we're searching for something—a clear path, a sign, or a way to know we're doing the right thing. We work hard, set goals, and chase success, but sometimes we still feel lost or uncertain. What if I say the answer we're looking for is already within us?

The eternal guide is the quiet voice inside us that always points us in the right direction. It's not something we can hear loudly or see clearly, but it's always there, helping us make decisions, find purpose, and stay true to who we are. This guide isn't something we need to search for—it's been with us all along.

So many times, we look outside of ourselves for guidance, thinking we need to find the right person or the right situation to show us the way. But the truth is, we already have everything we need. Our inner voice, our instincts, and our soul's direction are what we truly need to follow.

In this chapter, we'll explore how to connect with that inner guide—the part of us that knows exactly what we need to do. When we learn to trust our intuition and listen to that still, quiet voice, we begin to feel more confident about the choices we make and the path we walk.

It's not always about working harder or chasing after things we think we need. It's about finding peace in the fact that we have an inner guide showing us the way. The more we trust it, the clearer our journey becomes.

The eternal guide isn't far away—it's a part of us. This chapter will help you recognize it and trust it, so you can move forward with confidence, knowing that the right path is already inside you.

Listening to the Soul's Call

In the rush of life, it's easy to feel lost or uncertain about the future. We often search for answers outside ourselves—in other people, situations, or achievements. But what if the most important answers are already within us?

The Bhagavad Gita teaches us that our soul holds the wisdom we need. It knows the path we are meant to walk, and it quietly guides us toward our true purpose.

The eternal guide is the inner voice, the voice of the soul that speaks in the moments of stillness, through our intuition and in the gentle whispers of our heart. It's not a loud, dramatic voice but a quiet, steady guide that helps us make choices aligned with who we truly are. When we learn to listen, we realize that the answers to many of our questionshave been there all along.

In the Bhagavad Gita, Arjuna is confused and unsure about his duty. He looks for answers everywhere—in the opinion of others, in his emotions, and in his doubts. But it is only when he turns inward, listens to the wisdom of Lord Krishna, and aligns himself with his soul's purpose that he finds clarity and strength. Just like Arjuna, we must also turn inward to find our true direction.

Trusting your inner guide is not always easy. The path it reveals is often unfamiliar, and it may not align with what others expect. But the greatest breakthroughs in life happen when we dare to follow what feels right deep within. The Bhagavad Gita reminds us that every person has their own Dharma, a unique duty or purpose. Living according to this path brings not only success but also deep contentment.

Think of the Sun—it rises every day without questioning its role. It doesn't compare itself to the stars or the moon. It simply fulfills its purpose, bringing light and life. In the same way, when you trust your inner guide and focus on your unique path, you shine effortlessly.

Steps to tune into your guide:

1. Quiet the mind: Spend time in silence daily—through meditation, deep breathing, or simply sitting still. This helps you hear your inner voice.

2. Follow your intuition: Trust your instincts even when the path seems uncertain; your first feeling is often the soul's nudge.

3. Stay consistent: Revisit your inner guide regularly; consistency strengthens your connection to it.

4. Accept challenges as lessons: View obstacles as opportunities for

growth, not as roadblocks. Every challenge knocks the door of growth.

5. Practice gratitude: Acknowledge the guidance you receive and be thankful for the clarity it brings.

When you align with your eternal guide, life doesn't become perfect, but it does become purposeful. Challenges don't feel like obstacles; they are stepping stones. Success is no longer about impressing others—it's about staying true to yourself. The peace that comes from this alignment is what the Gita calls liberation—freedom from the chaos of doubt and confusion.

Your eternal guide is waiting. Trust it, and let it lead you to a life of clarity, strength, and unshakable purpose.

Your Inner Intuition:

In the fast-paced world we live in, it's easy to feel overwhelmed by noise—opinions of others, expectations, and even our own doubts. But beyond all this, there's a quiet, steady voice within us that knows the right path. This is your inner intuition, your true guide. The Bhagavad Gita teaches us that this inner voice is the connection to your higher self—the soul's wisdom that leads you toward purpose and fulfillment.

In the Gita, Arjuna stands on the battlefield of Kurukshetra. Paralyzed by doubts and fear, he doesn't know what to do or which path to take. In that moment of crisis, Krishna reminds him to focus inward and trust his Dharma—his true purpose. Krishna tells him, "Your own duty, though imperfectly performed, is better than the duty of another well performed."

This profound teaching encourages us to listen to our intuition, even if the road ahead seems uncertain or difficult.

Your inner intuition is not loud or forceful; it's a whisper, a gentle nudge.In the right direction, it speaks when you're quiet. The Gita emphasizes that your actions should come from your inner self, not from greed or the need to please others. Your intuition is that inner self speaking to you. It knows what you need, even when your mind is full of doubts. Trusting your intuition doesn't mean the path will always be easy, but it will always feel right.

Think of it as a compass—it might not give you the entire map, but it points you in the right direction. The more you follow it, the clearer the path becomes. Just like Arjuna had to trust Krishna's wisdom and take action, you too must trust your inner guide and take steps toward purpose.

Your inner intuition is your connection to something greater—it's the soul's way of guiding you toward a life of purpose, peace, and strength. Trust it, follow it, and let it lead you to your highest potential, just as Krishna guided Arjuna.

Your inner intuition is always there. Trust the whisper within, and you will find the courage to live a life of meaning and clarity.

Walking the Path of Purpose

Life is full of choices, challenges, and crossroads. In these moments, we often wonder: What is the right path for me? The answer lies Discovering and following your dharma—your true purpose. Your dharma isn't about external rewards or comparisons; it's about aligning your actions with your inner values and living authentically.

Take the story of Karna from the Mahabharata. Born with unmatched talent and strength, Karna's life was a series of struggles—rejected for his origin, insulted for his status, and denied opportunities because of societal prejudice. Despite these hardships, Karna stayed true to his purpose. He honed his skills as a warrior, stood by his principles, and remained loyal to those who believed in him.

Karna's life teaches us that living with purpose isn't about the circumstances you are born into—it's about the choices you make. Even when the odds are against you, your commitment to your truth defines your path.

Dharma is not just about duty; it's about living in alignment with your true self. It's not always easy—sometimes it means standing alone, going against the grain, or making sacrifices. But it's through these challenges that you find your strength and clarity.

The story of Karna is not just about struggle; it's about resilience, courage, and the power of living your truth. No matter where you start, your dharma will guide you to loge of significance. Trust your path , embrace your purpose and let your life shine with meaning and strength.

The art of surrender

Life often teaches us that the more we try to control everything, the more frustrated we become. We plan, we push, we expect—but when things don't go our way, we feel lost. True strength doesn't come from endless struggle; it comes from learning when to act and when to let go. This is the art of surrender—giving your best while trusting that the universe will take care of the rest.

Many think surrender means weakness or giving up, but it's the opposite. Surrender is a conscious choice to release the need for absolute control. It means accepting that while we can put in the effort, the outcome is not always in our hands. The sun doesn't rush to rise, yet It always appears at the right time. Rivers do not force their way, yet they reach the ocean. Nature thrives by flowing, not by fighting. We too must learn this wisdom.

Surrender doesn't mean you stop working hard—it means you stop worrying unnecessarily. It means walking forward with faith, knowing that whatever is meant for you will find you at the right time. Let go of control, embrace the flow, and trust that your journey is unfolding perfectly.

-----------------**Chapter Summary**----------------------

- Your path is shaped by your choice, not external circumstances.
- Trust the quiet voice within; it guides you toward what is right for you.
- Stay committed to your journey even when challenges arise. Purpose is built through action.
- Give your best but release the need to control everything. True power lies in trusting the process.
- Move forward with confidence, trusting the process.

VII

The Silent Archit

Every skyscraper begins with an invisible blueprint. Every masterpiece starts in the mind of its creator. Your life is no different. You are the Silent Architect of your destiny, shaping it with every thought, belief, and decision you make.

Your thoughts are not just passing whispers; they are the silent forces shaping your future. What you believe, you become. What you focus on, you attract. Every decision, every habit, every mindset—these are the bricks building your reality.

The difference between those who lead and those who follow is simple—leaders don't wait for destiny; they build it, while others drift, hoping for change. Winners take control, design their future, and make it happen.

Your thoughts are not just whispers in your mind; they are commands to your reality. What you think, you become. Think weak, and life will break you. Think strong, and nothing can stop you. The greatest battles are not fought in the world—they are fought within your own mind. Fear vs. Faith. Doubt vs. Confidence. Hesitation vs. Action.

The moment you decide to master your thoughts, you take full control of your destiny.

So ask yourself: Are you shaping your life, or is life shaping you? belongs to those who dare to design their future. Think bold. Act fearless. Become unstoppable.

The Blueprint of Belief

Every building stands on a foundation, and every destiny is built on belief. Your beliefs are the silent architects of your future. They decide what you chase, what you settle for, and what you believe is possible. If you don't control them, they will control you.

Most people live inside mental walls built by fear, doubt, and limitations. They inherit beliefs from society, past failures, or the opinions of others. But champions don't accept a reality they didn't design. They break the old blueprint and create their own.

Your mind is a battlefield, and belief is your greatest weapon. If you believe in failure, you will find reasons to quit. If you believe in success, you will find a way forward, no matter the odds. Greatness is not given; it is built, brick by brick, belief by belief.

History has never been written by those who doubt themselves. Every great leader, visionary, and warrior had one thing in common—unshakable belief. They saw possibilities where Others saw obstacles. They refused to bow to fear. They designed their destiny before the world could shape it for them.

It's time to ask yourself: Are your beliefs working for you or against you? Are you following a blueprint designed by fear, or are you creating one built on faith and strength? Tear down anything that weakens you. Destroy every thought that tells you you're not good enough. Rebuild your mind with confidence, vision, and resilience.

The world belongs to those who believe in something greater—those who believe in themselves even when no one else does. The choice is yours. Will you live by default, or will you design your destiny?

The Power of Inner Dialogue

There is a voice inside you that never stops speaking. It is there when you wake up, when you take risks, when you hesitate, and when you decide to push forward.

This voice—your inner dialogue—is the silent force shaping your destiny. Every champion, every leader, every visionary has mastered this voice.They have trained their inner dialogue to be their greatest weapon, not their greatest enemy. While others drown in self-doubt, they fuel their minds with words of power, strength, and unshakable belief.

Your mind is always listening. If you tell yourself you are weak, unworthy, or not ready, your mind will find reasons to prove you right. You will hesitate, you will hold back, and you will watch opportunities pass you by. But if you tell yourself you are strong, capable, and destined for greatness, your mind will move mountains to make it true.

Most people don't fail because they lack talent or resources. They fail because they lose the battle within. They let fear whisper louder than courage. They let doubt speak louder than confidence. But those who rise, those who win, have one thing in common: they control the voice inside. They silence fear. They reject doubt. They command their mind to work for them, not against them.

Every word you say to yourself is a brick in the foundation of your future. Speak weakness, and you build a life of hesitation. Speak strength, and you build an empire of confidence.

What you tell yourself is your hardest moment determines whether you break or rise.

So ask yourself: what kind of conversation are you having with yourself? Are you speaking power, or are you feeding fear? Reprogram your mind. Train your inner dialogue to be your greatest motivator, your strongest ally, your most loyal supporter. Because in the end, the voice that speaks the loudest inside you will determine the life you build outside.

It's time to take control. Speak with strength. Think with power, turn your inner voice into the force that drives you towards greatness.

Mastering the mind:

Your mind is the most powerful tool you will ever own. It can either build you into a person of strength, focus, and success—or trap you in a cycle of doubt, distraction, and failure. Mastering the mind is not about stopping thoughts but about controlling them. It's about choosing discipline over impulse, focus over distraction, and clarity over chaos.

Most people live as slaves to their minds. They let fear dictate their actions, emotions, cloud their decisions, and distractions steal their time. They react to life instead of directing it. But those who master their minds understand one truth: your thoughts shape your reality. A disciplined mind moves with intention. It stays steady in storms, focused in chaos, and unstoppable in the face of challenges.

In the Bhagavad Gita, Lord Krishna says: "For one who has conquered the mind, the mind is the best of friends. But for one who has failed to do so, the mind will remain the greatest enemy." This means that if you control your thoughts, your mind will guide you toward success. But if you let your mind run wild, it will pull you away from your goals, filling you with self-doubt, fear, and distractions.

Mental discipline is built in small everyday choices. It's the decision to wake up early instead of hitting snooze. It's the ability to stay focused on your work instead of mindlessly scrolling on your phone. It's choosing to keep going even when things get hard. The stronger your mind, the stronger your decisions, the stronger your life.

A disciplined mind doesn't mean you don't feel emotions. It means you don't let emotions control you. It means staying calm under pressure, thinking logically instead of reacting impulsively, and making choices based on long-term vision instead of temporary feelings.

Training your mind is like training a muscle; the more you practice, the stronger it becomes. Start by becoming aware of your thoughts. Are they empowering you or limiting you? Are they focused or scattered? Are they helping you grow or keeping you stuck?

"Rule your mind, or it will rule you." – Buddha

The Warrior's focus

In the world filled with noise, true warriors are those who master their focus. They do not allow distractions to pull them away from their path. They walk with clarity, act with purpose, and remain unshaken by chaos. This is the essence of the Bhagavad Gita—to act without hesitation, to work without attachment, and to move with unwavering determination.

Lord Krishna tells Arjuna:
"The mind is restless, no doubt, but it can be controlled by practice and detachment."

This is the secret to supreme focus: consistency and detachment. Most people drift aimlessly because they allow their minds to be consumed by distractions—temptation, fears, and fleeting pleasure. But one who controls his mind controls his destiny.

Distraction is the greatest thief of time. It pulls you away from your purpose, scatters your energy, and weakens your will.
A warrior of life doesn't let his mind wander aimlessly; he directs it toward his goal like an arrow aimed at its target.

The more focused the mind, the more powerful the action. A focused mind is like a sharp sword—it cuts through confusion and doubt. Every great leader, thinker, and creator has one thing in common: they protect their focus.

Victory belongs to the one who stays steady, undisturbed by temptation, and committed to his duty.
In life, success does not come to those who chase everything; it comes to those who walk one path with unwavering focus.

------------------*Chapter Summary*---------------------

• 59 •

- Your mind is the architect of your future. Shape it wisely.
- True mastery begins with control. Your thoughts control your life.
- Inner discipline is the foundation of all achievements.
- The one who wins within wins everywhere.
- Your silent efforts today will become your greatness tomorrow.

VIII
The power of Hour

Success isn't about making big moves overnight. It's about small actions you take every single day. Whether you realize it or not, your habits are shaping your future. Every choice you make—waking up early or hitting snooze, reading for 10 min or scrolling social media—moves you closer or further from your goals.

Most people think success is about motivation, but let's be honest—motivation fades. You don't wake up feeling inspired every day. That's why relying on motivation is a losing game. The real winners? They rely on habits, not emotions. They set up their daily routines in a way that makes success automatic.

Now, imagine two people waking up in the morning. One jumps out of bed, spends the first hour focused—exercising, learning, planning the day. The other wakes up late, scrolls their phone, rushes through the morning. Fast forward a year—who do you think is ahead? The difference isn't talent, it's their habits.

The way you spend the first hour of your day sets the tone for everything else.

A strong routine builds momentum, clarity, and focus. It's like setting the right foundation for a house—if it's weak, everything else crumbles. That's why mastering your habits, especially in the morning, is a game changer.

But here's the problem—most people try to change everything at once. They wake up one day, make a long list of "good habits," and expect instant transformation. That's not how it works. Habits grow like compounding interest. Small, consistent changes create huge results over time.

The key to success isn't in doing more, but in doing the right things consistently. This chapter isn't about complex theories—it's about real, practical steps that you can use to build a system that works for you. This is your chance to change things. It's not about being perfect—it's about feeling in control of your time, one habit at a time.

The Habit Loop

Every day, you repeat countless actions without thinking—brushing your teeth, checking your phone, drinking coffee. These actions feel. Automatic because they are habits, deeply wired into your brain. But have you ever wondered how these habits form? Why do some behaviors stick effortlessly, while others fade away? The answer lies in The Habit Loop—a psychological pattern that controls how habits are created and reinforced.

Understanding this loop is the key to transforming your daily life. If you master this process, you won't need to rely on motivation or willpower. Instead, success will become a natural byproduct of your routine.

Understanding the Habit Loop:

Every habit—good or bad—follows the same pattern:

Cue (Trigger): A trigger that reminds you to act.
Ex: Seeing a book on your desk reminds you to write.

Routine (Action): The habit itself, the behavior you repeat.
Ex: You write for 10 minutes.

Reward (Outcome): The benefit your brain associates with it.
Ex: You feel accomplished.

At first, this cycle is a conscious choice. But over time, the brain automates it, making the habit effortless. This is why you instinctively reach for your phone in the morning or feel the need for coffee at a certain hour.

This loop is what drives behavior. If you understand it, you can create powerful habits that push you forward.

Small Actions, Big Impact

Let's say you want to write daily:

Cue: Set a reminder or keep your notebook visible and make the cue obvious.

Routine: Write for just 10 minutes and make the routine easy—not too much.

Reward: Allow yourself to enjoy a small win—maybe crossing it off a to-do list.

At first, it feels insignificant. But over weeks and months, it becomes effortless.
This applies to anything—fitness, learning, business, or personal growth.
Look at the world's greatest writers, entrepreneurs, or athletes. None of them rely on purely on motivation. They rely on habits to stay consistent.

Mastering the First Hour

The way you start your morning defines the rest of your day. Because the first hour of your day is like the foundation of a building—if it's strong, everything else stands firm. The first hour is your launch pad, setting the tone for your energy, focus, and success, and your entire day flows better. But if you wake up feeling distracted, rushed, or lost, your day will likely follow the same pattern.

Successful people don't leave their mornings to chance. They design them. They understand that the first hour sets the tone for everything that follows.

~ Why Morning Matters

Your brain is at its sharpest in the morning. After a night of rest, it's like a blank slate, ready to absorb new ideas and make strong decisions. But the first thing you do in the morning determines the direction of your momentum.

It's like a domino effect—one strong push in the right direction and everything falls into place. If your first actions involve focus and clarity, your mind follows that pattern. If they involve stress and distraction, your entire day becomes scattered.

~ Take Control of Your Mornings

Mastering the first hour isn't about perfection; it's about consistency. Here's a simple yet powerful way to build a routine that works:

Move your body – The moment you wake up, stretch, walk, or do a quick workout. This wakes up your system and signals it's time to be ready for the day.

Feed your mind – Instead of mindlessly scrolling, read something inspiring, write in a journal, or practice gratitude. Your first thoughts shape your mindset.

Plan your day – Clarity is power. Define your top three priorities for the day—don't just "go with the flow," direct it.

Avoid Morning Traps – The worst habit? Checking your phone first thing. Social media, emails, and notifications hijack your focus before you've even set your own intentions.

Be Grounded – Many of history's great minds, philosophers, leaders, and visionaries started their mornings with silence, reflection, or prayers. This isn't just a ritual; it's about grounding yourself before the world demands your attention. Whether through meditation, deep breathing, or gratitude, connecting with yourself in the first hour builds resilience, focus, and peace.

You don't need a perfect morning routine—you just need an intentional one. Even small changes like five minutes of stretching, a quick journal entry, or setting one clear goal can transform your energy and focus.

The Shadow of Habit

Our life is not shaped by big moments but by the small actions we repeat every day. Just like shadows follow us everywhere, habits quietly influence our choices, mindset, and future. They work in the background—sometimes pushing us forward, sometimes holding us back.

A habit is more than just an action; it becomes part of who we are. A person who reads daily is a reader. Someone who exercises regularly is an athlete in spirit. The things we do consistently shape our identity, even if we don't notice it. Success doesn't come from one big effort—it comes from the small things we do over and over again.

~ The Unseen Power of Habit

Think about a river carving through a rock. It doesn't happen overnight. But over time, the steady flow of water changes the shape of the rock completely. Habits work the same way. Small, daily actions might seem unimportant today, but they slowly create a new version of you.

Good habits build you up, while bad habits slowly pull you down. Procrastination, negativity, and unhealthy choices don't destroy us in a single day. But like a shadow growing longer in the evening, their effects grow silently until they become hard to change. The scary part? Most of the time, we don't even realize how much our habits are shaping us.

How to Take Control

The first step to mastering habits is awareness. Just like a shadow needs light to exist, our habits exist because of our routines and surroundings. Pay attention to what triggers your habit. Do you reach for your phone out of boredom? Do you skip workouts because you feel tired? Once you understand what's driving your habits, you can start changing them.

Replace bad habits with better ones. If you waste time on your phone, try reading a book instead.

Make good habits easy. Keep a water bottle near you to drink more water. Lay out workout clothes the night before.

Start small. Big changes don't happen in a day. Even 1% improvement every day leads to massive results over time.

Habits are powerful. They shape your future without you even realizing it. You have the power to step into the light and build the habits that will take you forward. Success. Small actions create a big change. So, choose them wisely.

The power of small things.

Success is not about huge changes but small, consistent improvements. A 1% shift in your daily habits may seem tiny, but over time, it can lead to a completely different destination in life—just like a flight changing its course by a few degrees.

Imagine a plane taking off from Delhi to Bengaluru. If the pilot adjusts the course by just 2 degrees south, you will land in Chennai instead of Bengaluru. Such a small shift at the beginning creates a massive difference in the final destination.

This is how habits work. A small good habit, like writing a page daily, may not seem significant today, but in a year, it can result in a complete book. Similarly, a small bad habit, like hitting snooze every morning, can lead to lost opportunities over time.

Brushing for 30 seconds extra daily protects your teeth for years.

Walking 1,000 extra steps a day improves health over time.

Reading for 10 minutes daily makes you wiser in a year.

The Echo of Action

Every action we take leaves an imprint—not just on the world around us but within ourselves, like a ripple in still water. Habits and choices echo far beyond the moment they occur. The life you are living today is the result of past actions, and the life you will live tomorrow depends on what you choose today.

Success and failure are rarely instant; they are the result of repeated patterns. A small habit, repeated daily, might seem insignificant, but over time, it shapes your character, mindset, and destiny. Just like a seed takes time to grow into a tree, our habits slowly but surely carve the path we walk.

The Bhagavad Gita teaches us that action, or Karma, is never wasted—it always has a consequence. Whether positive or negative, every effort compounds. If we cultivate discipline today, it will reward us in the future. If we allow distractions to control us, we will face the consequences later.

The question is: What kind of echo do you want to leave behind? Are your daily actions bringing you closer to your vision, or are they leading you astray ? The power to shape your future is in your hands. One small action at a time.

----------------*Chapter Summary*----------------

- Your first hours shape your entire day. Start with purpose, not distractions.

- Morning habits create momentum. A structured routine fuels focus and discipline.

- The loop of habit strengthens success. Small repeated actions become automatic over time.

- The echo of action creates a lasting impact. Even the smallest step today can shape your future.

- Win the morning, win life. Productive mornings lead to success. A well-structured start sets the tone for everything that follows.

- Success isn't about sudden transformation—it's about tiny, consistent changes that shape your future.

• 69 •

IX

The Daily key

"People do not decide their futures, they decide their habits and their habits decide their future."– F.M. Alexander

Success is not about luck or shortcuts—it's about consistency, patience, and belief in the journey. Life often tests us with distractions, failures, and moments of doubt. In these times, two things keep us moving forward: focus & faith.

Focus means staying committed to your goal, no matter what comes your way. It's about choosing what truly matters and avoiding distractions. But focus alone isn't enough—you also need faith, the trust that your efforts will pay off, even when results aren't immediate.

Imagine planting a seed. You water it daily even when you don't see instant growth. With time, patience, and care, it eventually turns into a strong tree. Success works the same way. Small, consistent efforts may seem insignificant at first, but they build a strong foundation over time.

By embracing this blend of focus and faith, you can turn everyday struggles into stepping stones for success. Let's embark on this journey to build that bridge—one that carries you through obstacles and leads you to a future filled with purpose and achievement.

Living with Persistence

Success doesn't happen overnight—it takes time, effort, and patience. Persistence means not giving up, even when things get difficult. It is the key that helps people achieve their dreams, no matter how many obstacles come their way.

Life is full of challenges. Sometimes, things don't go as planned, and failure can feel discouraging. But those who succeed are the ones who keep going despite the difficulties. The real difference between successful and unsuccessful people is not talent—it is the ability to keep trying.

Think about a river carving through a rock. It doesn't happen overnight, but with continuous flow, the river shapes even the hardest stone. Your journey is the same—every small action, every bit of effort adds up over time.

One of the best examples of persistence is Thomas Edison. As the inventor of the light bulb, he failed over 1,000 times before successfully inventing it. But instead of seeing failure as a defeat, he saw it as a learning experience.

Once said, "I have not failed. I've just found 1000 ways that won't work." His determination led him to success.

But persistence is not just about working hard; it's about working smart. Being persistent doesn't mean blindly repeating the same mistakes. It means learning, adjusting, and staying committed. When something doesn't work, you refine your approach instead of giving up.

To build persistence, start with these three things:

1. A clear purpose – When you know why you're doing something, giving up isn't an option.

2. Learn from failure – Mistakes are part of the journey. Every failure teaches something valuable.

3. Daily discipline – Even small efforts add up over time. Consistency is more important than speed.

Success is not about avoiding difficulties; it is about facing them strong with a strong mindset. There will be ups and downs, but if you keep moving forward step by step, you will reach your goals.

Why Habits Matter

Habits shape our lives more than we realize. They are the small actions we do every day without thinking, like brushing our teeth, checking our phones, or even the way we react to challenges. Over time, these small actions add up and decide where we end up in life. Want to be successful? Build good habits. Want to stay stuck? Keep bad ones. Simple, right?

Now, let's make this fun! Imagine life as a road trip—your habits are the fuel. If you fill your car with clean, high-quality fuel (good habits), you will go far and reach amazing places. But if you pour in dirty, low-quality fuel (bad habits), your car will break down, and you'll be stuck on the side of the road. No one wants that!

Small Habits

The best part about habits? They don't need to be big. A 1% improvement every day might seem tiny, but over time, it leads to huge results. Think about learning a new skill—practice for just 10 minutes a day may not seem like much, but after a year, that's over 60 hours of practice! That's how habits work—they quietly shape us into better versions of ourselves.

The 1% Improvement

If you improve by 1% every day, the formula is:
$$1.01^{365} = 37.78$$

That means in one year, you become **37** times better than when you started.

A simple graph to visualize this effect:

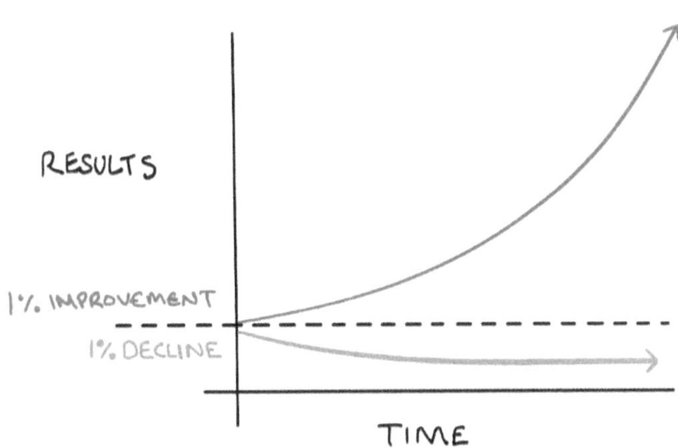

The straight line represents **1%** improvement daily, leading to **37×** growth in a year.

The dashed line represents **1%** decline daily, where progress drops close to zero.

Take successful people. They aren't born with superpowers. They just master the art of good habits—waking up early, staying disciplined, focusing on what matters, and continuously learning. Even athletes don't wake up one day and become champions. They train daily, eat right, and stay consistent.

Good habits don't just lead to success—they also make life more enjoyable. Waking up early gives you more time for your life, exercising makes you feel energetic, and reading every day expands your mind. These little things make a big difference in how happy and confident you feel.

And guess what? Building habits doesn't have to be boring. Reward yourself, make it fun, and enjoy the process. Want to start exercising? Play your favorite music while you do it. Trying to wake up early? Treat yourself to a great breakfast. The easier and more enjoyable a habit is, the more likely you are to stick with it.

At the end of the day, habits decide our future. Start small, stay consistent, and watch how your life transforms.

Trust the Process

In today's time, we are conditioned to expect instant results. We start a new habit, set a goal, or work on a project, and if we don't see immediate success, we feel discouraged. But real growth doesn't happen overnight. Success is not about speed; it's about consistency. This is why trusting the process is so important—it allows you to stay committed even when results seem invisible.

Think of a bamboo tree.
After planting the seed, for years, nothing appears above the ground. But beneath the surface, its roots are growing, spreading deep and growing stronger. Then, suddenly, in a short period, it shoots up, growing several feet in just a few weeks.

The years of unseen progress were never wasted; they were essential for strong growth. Life works the same way. Just because you don't see results immediately doesn't mean your efforts are not working.

Many people give up too soon because they don't trust the process. They switch paths, chase quick fixes, or get frustrated when success doesn't come fast enough. But if you

If you quit too early, you never allow your effort to compound. Small, consistent actions—like daily learning, disciplined habits, and steady effort—create powerful momentum over time.

Trusting the process doesn't mean waiting passively; it means believing in the power of small efforts. Every action you take is like planting a seed. Some will grow quickly, while others take time. If you stay patient, persistent, and focused, the result will come. Success is not a single event; it is the result of countless small steps taken with faith and determination.

So, when you feel like giving up, remember: keep going. The process is shaping you, strengthening you, and preparing you for great things.

------------*Chapter Summary*------------

- Success is a journey that requires both persistence and trust in the process.
- Habits play a crucial role in shaping our mindset and daily action.
- Challenges and setback are the part of growth overcoming them builds resilience.
- Discipline and faith go hand in hand staying committed leads to result.
- True success isn't about reaching goal, it's about who you become along the way.

X
Conclusion The journey within

Sucess is not just about external achievements. its about mastering your mind buildings , strong habits and align your action with purpose. this book has guided you through goal setting , time management , leadership and the silent power of habits. But the real journey begins within. Never undesestimate yourself. The smallest step in the right direction can change your entire destiny. Stay disciplined trust the process and be persistence. Small efforts taken consistently, create extraordinay results. you are far more capable than you think. Belive act, and watch your life transformation. The journey never ends; it only evolves keep walking your path with purpose.

Author's Note

Never stop, never settle. Life will test you, challenge you and try to hold you back, but never. You must keep moving forward. Sacrifice anything that stands between you and your goal – comfort, distractions, or even doubts. Success is not about how fast you reach your destination but about never quitting along the way.

Believe in yourself. Never underestimate your potential. The journey may be tough, but every step you take makes you stronger. Never think about what others think of you; their opinions don't define your journey. Keep pushing, keep evolving, and remember – your dreams are worthy of every effort.

Writing tihis book has been a journey of self discovery and growth. My goal is to share insights that inspire and help you on your path to success. I appreciate your time and hope this book adds value to your life.

Connects with me:

Instagram: harshbharti29

LinkedIn: Harsh Bharti

E mail: bhartiharsh990@gmail.com

References

1. **Atomic Habits** - James Clear *(Power of small habits, consistency)*

2. **Think and Grow Rich** - Napoleon Hill *(Persistence, power of belief)*

3. **The Power of Now** - Eckhart Tolle *(Mindfulness, staying present)*

4. **Bhagavad Gita** *(Inner wisdom, duty, resiliency in challenges)*

5. **The 7 Habits of Highly Effective People** - Stephen R. Covey *(Productivity, self-mastery)*

6. **Ignited Minds** - A.P.J. Abdul Kalam *(Dreams, discipline, vision for success)*

7. **The Power of Mind** - Swami Vivekananda *(Mental strength, control over thoughts)*

8. **Meditation and Its Methods** - Swami Vivekananda *(Spiritual discipline, focus, self-awareness)*